# Why Can't I Be The Boss Of Me?

Written by B. Annye Rothenberg, Ph.D.
Child/Parent Psychologist

Illustrated by
Bonnie Bright

REDWOOD CITY, CALIFORNIA

## DEDICATION

*To the many parents who do all they can — and then even more — to raise their children well.*

*And to my grown-up son, Bret, who is the joy of my life. There is so much strength in the life-long loving bond between children and parents. Child rearing — challenging and so rewarding — is an amazing journey!*

—B.A.R.

*Text copyright © 2015 by B. Annye Rothenberg*
*Illustrations copyright © 2015 by Bonnie Bright*

Library of Congress Control Number: 2014956537
ISBN: 978-0-9790420-6-5 (pbk.)

Printed in Hong Kong          First printing September 2015
10  9  8  7  6  5  4  3  2  1

### Published by
PERFECTING PARENTING PRESS
REDWOOD CITY, CALIFORNIA
www.PerfectingParentingPress.com

**To order by phone, call:**
(810) 388-9500 (M-F 9-5 ET)
**For other questions, call:**
(650) 275-3809 (M-F 8-5 PT)

Children's book in collaboration with
*SuAnn and Kevin Kiser*
Palo Alto, California

Parents' manual edited by
*Caroline Grannan*
San Francisco, California

Book design by
*Cathleen O'Brien*
San Francisco, California

**About the Cover**
*These parents asked their 8-year old son to go upstairs and get going on his homework. As they come upstairs to join him, they are very disappointed to see what he is doing. He's focused on his screen time and he looks at his parents with an attitude. (Even their dog knows he has made a bad choice!)*

*To parents (and parenting guidance professionals):*

# • WHAT'S IN THIS BOOK FOR CHILDREN AND FOR PARENTS •

*This book,* Why Can't I Be the Boss of Me?, *is meant to help families with kindergartners to third-graders whose children behave as if they are entitled to have a great deal of say in the family.* It teaches you how best to guide your children so they can benefit from what you want them to learn at home, at school, and about the world they will live in. If your children don't listen to you and argue, negotiate, and become angry, rude and insulting, your family will get much useful relief and guidance from this book.

***Sometimes it's hard to accept that this is happening in your home.*** But if it sounds familiar, what you read here can teach you ***why and how*** to help your kids accept that parents are the leaders who guide the family. When children run the family, they won't benefit from all the teaching and guidance they need to become socialized and motivated adults.

Children may act like they're your equals or even believe they can exceed your authority. This commonly happens because current popular parenting theory has had unexpected consequences. When children behave this way with their parents, they often expect to be the boss of their peers as well, and may push limits disrespectfully with teachers and other adults. Parents feel frustrated, angry, and even guilty when they can't get their children to do what they're told.

***This book has two parts: a story for children and a guidance section for parents.*** The story for children tells of eight-year-old Ryan, who has been given so much freedom that he's furious, rude, and relentless when he doesn't get his way. His behavior is insulting and disrespectful to his parents. Finally, the parents start to take charge.

This guidance section for parents teaches how the outcome of the "child is equal to the parents" approach has affected families in unanticipated and unacceptable ways. You'll learn how much say to give to children and what to do if your child expects too much control over you, his parents. You'll see how to motivate children without bribing, ***and*** what the new and more effective consequences are. You'll see how to guide your child in dealing with his frustration and anger. New tools in working with your parenting partner are explained. Overall, the parent guidance section shows you how to raise your child in an effective and compassionate way so he listens better and understands why you expect the behavior you do. The parent section helps you gain skills – one step at a time. This is all about helping our children, increasing the enjoyment of family life, and preparing them for a good future.

— **Annye Rothenberg, Ph.D., Child/Parent Psychologist**

---

★ *This new guidebook, by Dr. Annye Rothenberg combines a great children's story with a practical, yet thorough and systematic, advice section for parents that we have come to love about Dr. Rothenberg's books. This one focuses on the steps that teach children how to accept their parents' leadership role in the family — using a compassionate and respectful parenting approach. Our son and our family have benefited greatly from the book and I recommend it to any parent who is in search of a sensible, non-dogmatic guide that will help them in their everyday life with their child.*

—**Evelyn Wildgans, mother of a 6-year-old boy and school teacher, Cupertino, CA**

It was Saturday morning, and I knew exactly what I wanted to do.

"Can we go to the Children's Museum?" I asked Mom.

"Not now, Ryan," Mom said. "Even though it's the weekend, we still have work to do. Is your room clean?"

"Almost," I mumbled. I went to my room, but I didn't feel like cleaning, so I decided to build with my Lego bricks.

Training Your Dog

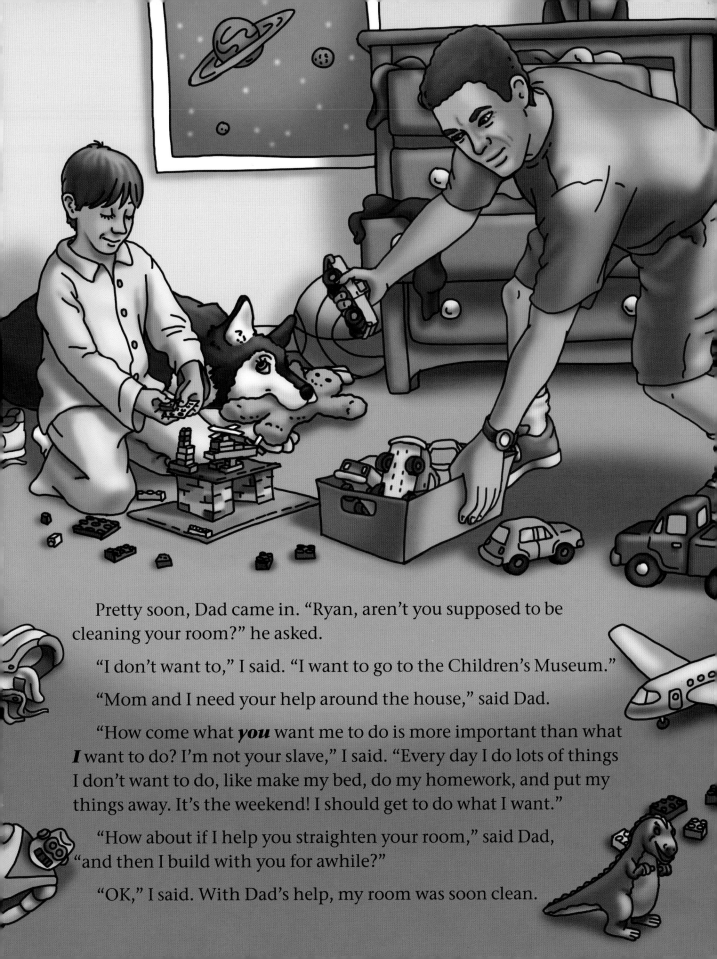

Pretty soon, Dad came in. "Ryan, aren't you supposed to be cleaning your room?" he asked.

"I don't want to," I said. "I want to go to the Children's Museum."

"Mom and I need your help around the house," said Dad.

"How come what **you** want me to do is more important than what **I** want to do? I'm not your slave," I said. "Every day I do lots of things I don't want to do, like make my bed, do my homework, and put my things away. It's the weekend! I should get to do what I want."

"How about if I help you straighten your room," said Dad, "and then I build with you for awhile?"

"OK," I said. With Dad's help, my room was soon clean.

"Now bring me the bag with the red Legos,"
I ordered Dad.

"If you say please," said Dad.

"Puh-leeeeeze!" I said.

Dad handed me a bag.

"I asked for the red *Legos*, not the red *bag*,"
I said, pouring out the yellow Legos. "Do these look
red to you?"

Dad got up and left my room.

"Where are you going?" I shouted.
"I still need your help!"

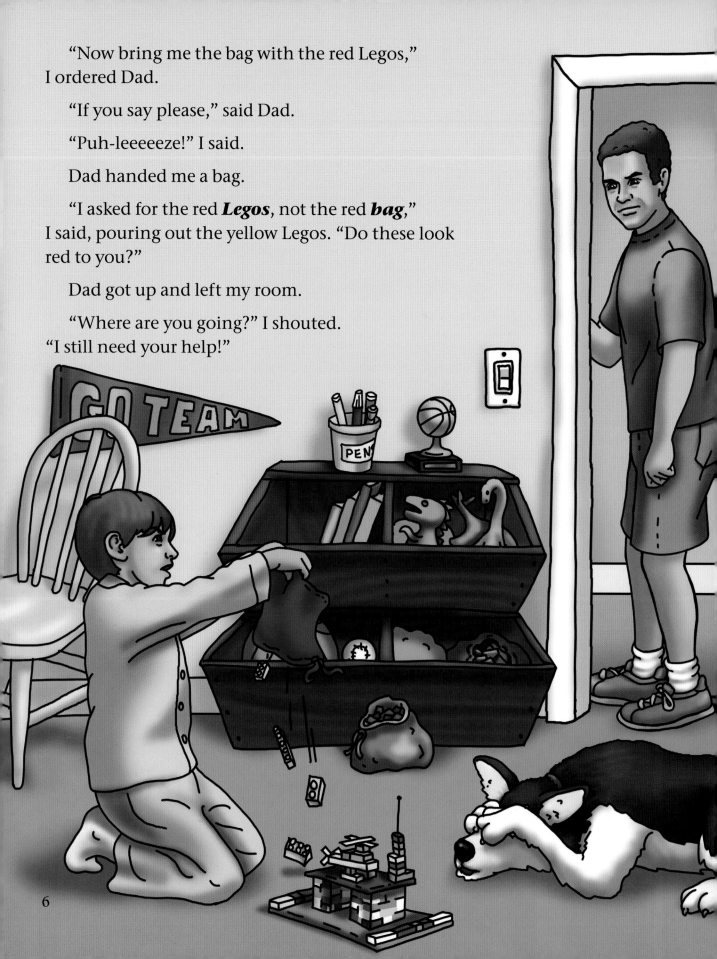

6

I heard Dad talking with Mom in the hall. Mom came in and said, "What's going on?"

"Dad said he would build with me after I cleaned up my room," I said, "but he walked out."

"I'm going to have you come food shopping with me," said Mom.

"I don't want to," I said. "If I can't go to the Children's Museum, I want to stay home and build with Dad."

"Dad just told me he needs a break from you," said Mom. "He thinks you're being rude."

"That's not fair," I said. "You both just want to boss me around. I should be the boss of me!"

"Kids always want to have their way," said Mom, "but that doesn't mean they should."

"OK," I said, "I'll go to the store with you, but only if I can play games on your phone while we're out."

"No, Ryan," said Mom. "You're not going to get your way every time. Now put on your shoes, and let's go."

At the supermarket, I tried to help Mom with the shopping.

On the ride home, Mom said, "Ryan, from now on, when you waste our time by arguing and trying to bargain with us, Dad and I are going to give you consequences. One of those consequences will be for you to do some of our chores."

"**What**!"

"When we get home, you will do my job of unloading the dishwasher and putting away the dishes," said Mom.

"You're so mean," I said.

"Saying that I'm mean is very rude, Ryan," said Mom. "Remember, I have a lot more jobs that I could give you."

Mom had her mad face on, and I didn't want even more jobs, so I didn't say anything else.

When we got home, Mom made lunch and I started to unload the dishwasher. Soon, Mom called Dad to have lunch.

"I want to eat now too," I said. "I promise I'll finish with the dishwasher later."

"No, Ryan," Dad said, "you have to finish your job first. If you hurry, you can still eat with us."

I finished the job much quicker than I thought I could, and ate lunch with Mom and Dad.

After lunch, we all went for a walk to the park.

"I want to get ice cream," I said.

"Not now, Ryan," said Dad.

"We have to teach you to listen to us," said Mom, "instead of just giving in to what you want."

"So, from now on," said Dad, "there will be new rules for you to follow."

"I bet they're stupid," I said.

Dad frowned. "What could you have said that wouldn't be rude?"

"I guess I could have said, 'I don't think I'm going to like your new rules'."

"Better," said Dad, "now repeat that three more times. The practicing-what-you-should-say consequence makes it easier to remember how to behave next time."

I didn't really want to say it three times, but I did anyhow.

"One new rule," said Mom, "is your homework must be done before dinner."

"Another is everyone will eat the same thing at dinner," said Dad.

"And another is you will only have screen time on the weekends," said Mom.

"Whoa," I said, "that sounds terrible!"

"We'll help you understand the reasons for these and our other new rules," said Dad.

"And we'll also help you learn how to make better decisions," said Mom.

"For example," said Dad, "before we eat out, we think about things like: how far away the restaurant is, how busy and noisy it is, when we last ate there, how healthy the food is, and how much it costs . . ."

"That's a lot to think about," I said.

"You'll learn eventually," said Mom, "and the better you get at making decisions, the more we'll respect your opinions."

"OK," I said, but I wasn't happy about not getting my way like I used to.

After our walk, Dad said, "Let's play a game together."

Mom read the rules out loud.

"This game has almost as many rules as you have for me!" I said.

Dad smiled. "Without rules, games would be impossible to play," he said. "Why do you think we have to teach you rules like putting away your clothes and toys and eating healthy foods?"

"Because parents are mean and don't want their kids to have any fun?"

Mom laughed. "I thought that too when I was a kid," she said. "Actually, we're teaching you rules because we want you to grow up to be someone who finds it easy to do the right thing at the right time, instead of thinking he should get to do whatever he wants."

"Just like you, we have to do things we don't want to do," said Dad, "like making dinner, fixing things that are broken, paying the bills, and cleaning out the garage."

"You mean grown-ups don't always get to do what they want?" I asked.

Dad shook his head. "No, being an adult is not like that. In fact, I have to make myself a list of things to do every day."

"I never knew that," I said. "Should I have a list of things to do every day?"

"That's a very good idea," said Mom. "Actually, I think you should have three lists: things to do before school, and after school, and right before bed."

"What about a weekend list?" I asked.

"Another good idea!" said Dad.

After we finished our game, Mom and Dad helped me make my lists, and we hung them in the kitchen, the bathroom, and my bedroom.

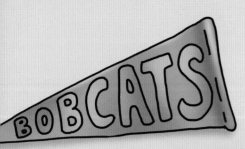

On Sunday morning, I hurried through my weekend list, checking off each chore as I did it. I hoped if I did a good job and finished quickly, Mom and Dad would take me to the Children's Museum.

"I'm done with my chores!" I said just before lunch.

"We've still got one big thing to do," said Dad.

"And it will probably take us all afternoon," said Mom.

"Oh, no," I groaned. I almost started to argue, but then I remembered what happened last time. "Maybe I can help," I said instead.

"You sure can," said Dad.

"Because the last item on our list," said Mom, "is...**take Ryan to the Children's Museum!**"

"Yay!" I shouted.

The museum was even better than I hoped. Dad and I built patterns and shapes in the Geometry Playground.

Mom and I petted sea creatures at the Tidal Pool.

19

All three of us danced and drummed and made music together.

But my favorite thing was a Food Science class I took all by myself.

That night after dinner, I said, "Today at the museum I learned how to make one of our favorite treats, and I want to show you how."

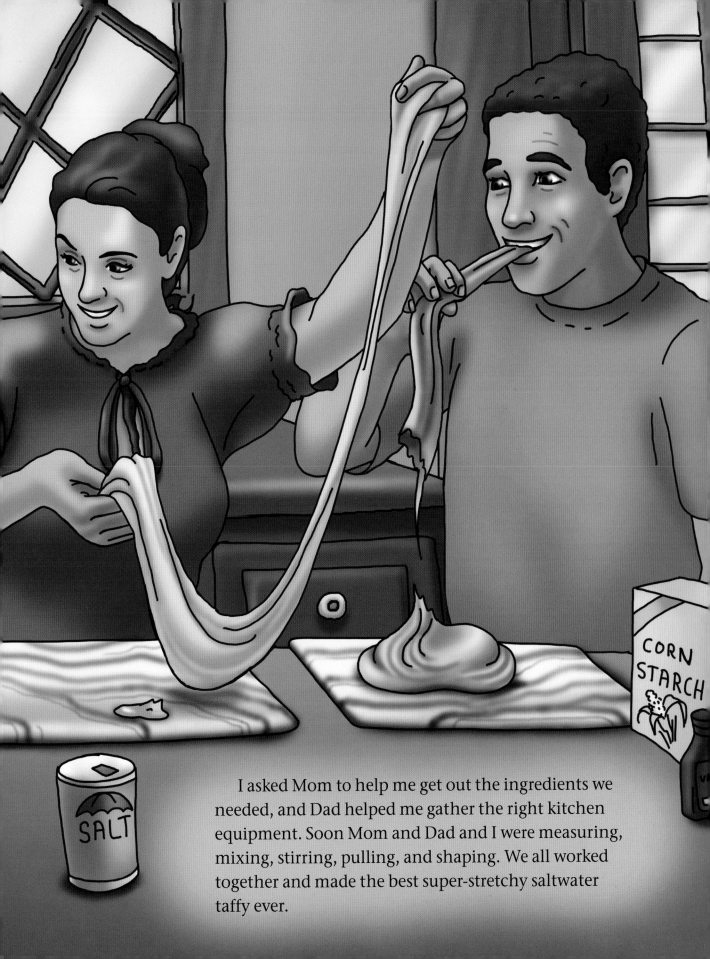

I asked Mom to help me get out the ingredients we needed, and Dad helped me gather the right kitchen equipment. Soon Mom and Dad and I were measuring, mixing, stirring, pulling, and shaping. We all worked together and made the best super-stretchy saltwater taffy ever.

I've learned a lot about making decisions since then.

Sometimes I get to be the boss of me, but it's best when Mom and Dad are in charge. We're all getting along way better now with them making the hard decisions and me just being a kid.

# A GUIDANCE SECTION FOR PARENTS

## Introduction

The is the *first book* in the series for *kindergartners through third-graders (five through eight-plus years old)* and their parents. (This author's previous six books are for parents and their three- through five-year-olds.) *This* book will help you know *how much you can expect of your elementary school child and how to guide and parent her\*, even if – and especially if – she believes she knows better than you do.*

An elementary school child's mind has developed to the point that she can be approached with logic and reason (e.g., "you took out all those things, so you're the one who needs to put them back"). Although children will still resist us, it's no longer because they are at the oppositional age (two through four years old). And we no longer have to make our requests sound fun and interesting, or talk through their teddy bears, to get them to respond. The five- to eight-year-old can make sense of our reasons, perspective, and logic, and can understand how her behavior affects us and how our consequences affect her.

By elementary school age, children's understanding of our roles and our reasons has matured. This is a relief to many parents who were frustrated when they tried to use reasonable explanations and logic with their preschoolers.

Five- to eight-year-olds are often a much easier age for parents. They can do all their basic care, such as dressing themselves. They are more responsible and don't have to be reminded about things as much. They are less impulsive, more careful about their own safety, and more aware of acceptable behavior. They can help out much more as members of the family. *However, there is a common concern that can still make these years a challenge.*

---

\* To avoid the awkwardness of "he or she," this book will use alternating genders section by section.

## When Children Expect Too Much Say and Control

Popular child-rearing guidance has swung from the authoritarian "do it because I said so" approach of forty-plus years ago to one that encourages parents to raise their children to have a great deal of say, promising that this approach builds children's self-esteem. *However, in many families, children have been given too much say and control, starting when the child is too young to make decisions – for example, asking a two-and-a-half-year-old what restaurant he wants to go to.* By the time children are school age, many parents, having used this approach with the best of intentions, continue down this path to avoid their child's emotional meltdowns, and theirs as well, even though they're not happy with the results. Children who are given too much say will resist what they need to learn from parents, teachers, and others. *Instead of being strengthened, children's self-esteem is diminished when their demand for control and their defiance make us frustrated and annoyed with them.*

If our kids don't believe they should listen to us and they argue, negotiate, and become furious with us when we don't let them have their way, we may not know how our parenting approach has contributed to their defiant behavior. We may not want to admit – even to ourselves – that we need to change our approach. *We don't want to just keep our fingers crossed that our children will grow out of this behavior.* We need to know what to do.

When parents have let their *preschooler* regularly choose the restaurant, the route to drive him to school, or the order of the parents' errands, this lays the groundwork for their *elementary school child* to expect to be a major decision-maker in the family and to be treated as an equal by the parents. Parents say that they would never have talked to their parents the way their children speak to them.

If your five- to eight-year-old believes he should have a lot of decision-making power in the family and gets annoyed and obnoxious *when you don't let him have his way, it's not too late to make the changes that will teach him why he can't be the boss of himself or of the family. Let's take this a piece at a time.*

## What to Expect of and Ask of our Five- to Eight-Year-Olds

When parents have regular routines for their kids to get ready for school, for meal and snack times, for homework, for screen time, for toy pick-up, for baths or showers, and for bedtime, there is usually much less pushback (limit-testing) by children. From kindergarten through third grade, here's what we can realistically expect our children to do:

### Getting up and getting ready

• Youngsters should get up easily in the morning, assuming they didn't go to sleep late. If we have to wake them in the morning, it means they haven't had enough sleep, so adjust their bedtimes so they can get the sleep they need (ten-eleven hours).

• They should know everything they have to do before school each morning. **Help your child** make a list in an order that he chooses **and** that works for the parents. If we simply impose a list on our kindergartners through third-graders, they're likely to be resistant. To set them up for success, **have them guess how long each step takes and then time them** and have them fill in those numbers – preferably on a non-rushed weekend day. They can join you in figuring out what time to get started in the morning to cut back on the nagging.

• Five- to eight-year-olds should be able to pick out clean, appropriate clothes and fully dress themselves. Kindergartners and first-graders often need you nearby in order to stay focused. Consider having them get dressed near you in the kitchen or in your bedroom so you can model keeping on task. Try to leave enough time so every minute before school doesn't require us to remind and rush them.

• Children will get through their list more willingly and with less nagging if they know that if they keep focused, they'll get free time before they leave for school. Screen-time activities should **not** be an option before school, because kids find those too hard to stop.

### Before leaving the house

• Children should leave their things in a reasonably organized manner, such as dirty clothes put where they belong, playthings put away except for those few projects that parents allow their kids to leave out, and beds made.

• They should have everything they need in their backpack. Most of this probably can be done the night before.

### After school

• **When school is over, kids need some snack time and playtime** followed by homework. Kids five to seven need close supervision to do homework; older children can usually do it at a desk in their room.

• They should have some free time in the afternoon and evening, although they may be have some days with scheduled after-school activities. **We want our kids to have some activities, but they shouldn't fill up all their after-school hours,** even if our child insists. Activities include sports, music, art, science, dance, second languages, and many other possibilities. After-school care is considered to be playtime.

• Playdates are worth encouraging. They offer another valuable type of socializing for kids who have been in groups all day.

• **At least an hour a day of heart-pounding exercise is very important.** If kids don't get that at recess, see how you can add it into the family activities so your children develop a positive attitude toward exercise – playing ball, going to the park, biking etc.

• In the evening, children should join the family for dinner, help with food preparation, and clear their own plates. There should be time for children to choose activities, play with siblings, and/or be with the family. Some children enjoy helping you with the dishes or laundry as ways to have time with you.

• Get into the habit of spending evenings with your child instead of catching up with work. When parents feel rushed and tired after work, they can be frustrated with how the time goes with their kids. However, some parents can work at home, stagger their work schedules, or have one parent work part time to handle this tension. (And, of course, there are still many families where one parent is an at-home parent.) **When we can't find a way to switch gears to be with our kids, they will often ignore, dawdle, or argue with us – just to get our attention.** Time together is better for kids than screen time or other solitary time, as it can fulfill everyone's emotional needs and builds the kind of closeness that enables children to want to more willingly accept their parents' guidance and values.

### Bedtime and sleep routines

• *Children should have the same bedtime each night.* Parents need to start the process at a regular time every evening. Children five to eight years old need ten to eleven hours of sleep a night, with the amount diminishing gradually.

• Beginning about 45 minutes before you want your child to fall asleep, the usual routines are: toy and project pick-up followed by a bath or shower; toothbrushing; toileting; pajamas; then into bed for the rest of the bedtime routine. Usually we're with our kids during these pre-bed steps until they're at least seven years old.

• The rest of the routine usually includes stories and chatting. (Children who are learning to read will relax more when they're read to at bedtime, but if your child wants to read to you, of course you should let her.)

• Five- to eight-year-olds should be able to fall asleep on their own and sleep through the night – except for

nightmares or sickness. About 80% can go through the whole night without getting up to use the toilet. (Try not to give them protein-rich food after dinner, such as milk or yogurt, because that can cause a need to urinate.*) Many still want their stuffed animals, and some want to read by themselves a little after you've left their room. Night lights are important to some children.

### What Should Five- to Eight-Year-Olds Be Able to Decide?

The first guideline is that a child should be able to decide only things *that affect him but do not create problems for him.* This means *he can decide* what clothes to wear, if he's dressed for the weather and the clothes aren't inappropriately styled or unkempt. *He can decide* what toy to play with or which activity to do at home (when there are no other responsibilities expected of him), but not if it causes problems for the rest of the family (too noisy, too dangerous, too addictive).

The second guideline is that he *shouldn't be making decisions that affect others,* such as whether he clears his project or homework off the table where you're about to have dinner, or where the family goes for vacation. Many easygoing parents say it doesn't bother them if their child wants things his way. But if our kids want to jump on the couch or refuse to pick up their toys

*The urine-suppressant hormone known as antidiuretic hormone (ADH) slows urine production at night, but protein foods put a heavy load on the kidneys, thus working in opposition to ADH, and cause an increase in the need to urinate.

or dirty clothes, and that doesn't bother us – *it should!* We have to raise our kids so their behavior is acceptable to society. Otherwise, they'll be corrected a lot by many adults and even by other children. This takes a toll on their relationships with others and on how they feel about themselves. Parents *inadvertently* make kids' lives harder by not taking **societal standards** into account, and also by not being selfish enough. Being a little selfish helps children accept that they can't always be first or be loud, and can't have most things their way. (This is known as *positive selfishness*, a tool parents can utilize to raise more considerate children.)

## How to Be an Authoritative Parent: Not Too Strict and Not Too Soft

Parents have to set rules for kids, and most children test these rules, these limits. Parents know they have to get their children to listen to them. They wonder how strict to be.

*Being very strict is much less common and much less acceptable today than in the past. Very strict* was when an an immediate "yes sir" or "yes ma'am" was required, and parents almost never explained themselves. It was a "you do it because I said so" era. Parents didn't care to hear your thinking, your excuses, or your feelings. *Today's parents want their children to be heard.* Many parents feel that they grew up in a family – although maybe not that strict – where they did what their parents said and didn't talk back. Many very strict families used physical punishment; others used fear tactics and possibly humiliation, none of which are considered acceptable today.

Today's parents want their children to listen to them but want to treat their children with more respect. It has been hard to know how to do that without elevating their young children almost to the status of equals, *letting them have a lot of say, impact, and control in what they do and even in what the family does.* Parents who allow this inadvertently train children to expect to have a huge influence on the rules. When a child's behavior and expectations go beyond the pale, as they commonly do, parents finally have to take back the parental power. This frustrates and outrages their children. Children – at that point – can seem so furious,

self-centered, and disrespectful that parents feel they have made some huge mistakes. They wonder what changes to make in their relationship to their children, and if it is too late. *It isn't!* You can make the changes, including learning new and improved consequences that are the keys to getting to the middle – not too strict or too soft – in your parenting. Knowing how she thinks and what you can expect of her at this age enables you to have a confident relationship with your child. You can't just give children orders every time you think of something you want them to do. Children don't respond well to commands.

## Helping Kids Understand Decision-Making

We want our kids to know why grownups will need to make many of the final decisions and show them how we make those decisions. And we don't want to just say to our kids, "This is something only parents decide," because we want to use decisions (small or large) as teaching opportunities. This way we don't just shut our kids down, which will likely be too jarring and infuriating to the child who has already had too much say for his age and has trouble listening to you. One way to teach your child about decision-making and *to show him that you are interested in his views on the issues you're deciding is to ask him to explain his reasoning.**

Often children who want to make the decisions have not been expected to give serious, logical thought to why it should be their way. They argue based on emotion rather than the logic and reason that they are now capable of. For example, the boy next door invites your child to play outside. *This is what might happen if both parent and child believe that the child has the right to have his way:* You tell him there's not enough time, because dinner will be ready in ten minutes. *He says that's enough time.* You say it isn't. He promises that he'll come in when you call him, and you let him go out to play. But when you call him, he argues: "That wasn't ten minutes. Jonah doesn't have to go in yet, so why do I? You don't care what I think. You're mean!"

Children do this a lot, annoying parents by resisting, blaming us, and seeing only their side. Now everyone is

---

* This is a thought-provoking question; these help children become better thinkers and problem-solvers.

upset. We can change this by asking children to give the reasons for their view, which also improves their reasoning ability. It's probably best to wait till tempers have cooled for the follow-up discussion, then ask your child to give you several reasons why he thought going out to play ten minutes before dinner sadly turned out to be a problem. (The reasons could be that he'd have to stop playing just when he's starting to have fun; that we need to eat when dinner is ready; that dinner can't be ready for each person at different times; that your family's rule is to eat together when everybody's home; and that we have a lot of things to do after dinner.) Then see if he can figure out some ways he can get more time with Jonah soon. We want to help him learn to reason better so he can be *a better thinker and a more considerate person.*

You can also talk to him about why he gave you all those justifications for playing outside longer: "You thought of lots of reasons I should let you keep playing with Jonah, but there were many reasons you needed to stop." This way, he learns that you hear him and understand him, but that these are grownup decisions. He can also benefit from brainstorming what he can say to his friend and himself when this happens again: "I can't come outside now because we're about to eat dinner, and it would be a problem for our family if we had dinner late." We use this process to help him start accepting that for good reasons, he can't continue having decision-making power for issues involving others.

*Children don't realize how much is involved in making good decisions.* Review what the parents said in the children's story about picking a restaurant (see p. 13). There are many decisions parents have to be in charge of – daily living decisions such as what food is kept in the house, screen-time rules, acceptable ways to treat each other, and what time bedtime is, and less common ones such as choosing vacations, cars, schools, and homes. As an example, tell your child about the factors that parents consider when deciding on a vacation: Do they want to go to a new place or an old favorite? Do they want to hike, lie on the beach, tour historic sites, visit extended family? Will everyone in the family like it? How much time is there for the trip? And don't forget getting there and getting home, lodging, the budget, babysitting, safety, passports, and immunizations. All this helps children realize how much there is to think about that's

beyond their experience, which explains why parents should make many of the decisions. But we also want to encourage their input, *if they give their reasons, because we want to support their ability to make more decisions as they get older.* However, make sure you tell your child that parents need to make the final decision so his expectations aren't crushed at the end.

Of course, five- to eight-year-olds see things simply and jump to conclusions quickly. If they hear about someone's cool vacation or car, they may decide that it's the perfect thing. They're sure their idea is great and are much less able to consider all that an adult would. We need to help them little by little to learn the big picture. We want our children to become good thinkers and decision-makers, aware that for now they should rely on us and our life experience, rather than frequently insisting that they know better than we do about decisions that affect the whole family.

## Why Children Think Parents Should Say Yes

*A child with an inflated view of the importance of her wants and opinions finds it much harder to get along with her family, as well as with other adults and peers.* Therefore, it's essential to work on reducing your child's overgrown expectations at home. If you go too far in letting her decide things *or* if you over-apologize (*"I'm really sorry,* but today I have to decide what's for dinner") or act guilty when a disappointing situation arises (*"It was my fault* for not reminding you to bring your cleats to soccer practice"), she will expect you to make her happy by saying yes to everything. Of course, children are most likely to think parents will say yes *if* we have given in partway or all the way at their insistence. *Before we tell them what we want them to do, we should say to ourselves, "What are my reasons for asking that?"* For our kids to respect us, we should rarely give in, and when we do, we should explain the reason: "You know what your bedtime is. The only reason it was later tonight was because the neighbors came over with an emergency."

Here's another example: Your child refuses to eat the chicken, broccoli, and rice you're making for dinner, and demands macaroni and cheese. If you give in, she learns she has the right to override your decisions and

## Building a Good Parent-Child Relationship

A successful parent-child relationship also requires our conversation, time, and affection in between all the many things we do and expect them to do. *As we go about our days, we want to make time to hear about what they're interested in and share things from our day that may interest them*. We need to reminisce about things we and they have both experienced and to make plans. Asking about things from yesterday helps children know we remember what they've said, showing them we're listening. *We should talk about things that are and aren't going well – at home, school, and elsewhere, for them and us.* (However, it's not helpful to criticize and correct them while telling them how perfect you were or are.) Make time to do projects or go on outings. Conversation, time, and affection show your child you really care about him. This makes it easier for a child to feel supported, loved, and connected to you, and interested in pleasing you.

*As your child grows and you expect more of him, you should tell him what's behind the new things you want him to do.* For example, explain why he'll be doing his homework at the desk in his room instead of at the kitchen table – because he needs less supervision and his homework requires more concentration – or why he'll be managing the recycling at home – because he's old enough and strong enough now.

When he does a job well, to help him feel proud of becoming more capable, tell him – if he's six – "you did that like a seven-year-old." Children are also more willing to take on increased responsibilities if they have increased privileges – staying up later, going down the street on their bike, having more say in planning the family outing, getting their allowance raised.

To improve your role as a respect-worthy parent, review with him what you should expect at his age. Make sure he knows why those things are his responsibility. Keep him updated as you add to the list. *Most important, before you tell him what you want from him, you have to mean it and remind yourself of your reasons.* Expect your child to try to convince you that he knows better than you why he shouldn't have to do that – *or* do it the way you wanted *or* do it without your help – now or ever.

to expect you to give her what she wants, now and in the future. Instead, *ask her the reasons* why *you* are making chicken, broccoli, and rice. Encourage her to give you several reasons. Tell her to "think harder" if she says she doesn't know. Ask her what problems there will be for you, the rest of the family, and her if you give her mac'n'cheese. (For example, it takes you extra time to make it, it's not as healthy, and her sibs may demand mac'n'cheese or other special food too.) *If she still refuses to eat what you're making, she should be expected to sit at the table with the family*. She can decide whether to try the food after all, or she can eat nothing and be hungry that evening, *since there won't be a snack later*. Most children will eat some of the meal rather than go hungry once they realize that for good reasons they aren't going to get their way. *If you give in to her demand to avoid fighting this battle, you are parenting only for the short term rather than the long term.* Then your child will believe you will cave at least partway in the future, and she will demand and argue for her way even more strongly.

Parenting *for the short term means taking the path of least resistance at the moment.* Parenting for the long term is *more effort now but is effective in getting your child to accept your rules*, and believe you have good reasons for what you say *and that you're respect-worthy.*

Don't let children's reactions to your requests mislead you into believing you're asking too much or not respecting them (e.g., "Why do I have to do all the work in the house?"). *You do know better than they do about what is best for them.* We have to feel confident that *we have both the right and responsibility to teach them what children their age should do and shouldn't do.* Children raised with a confident, caring, respect-worthy parent will develop the inner discipline we all want for our kids. This includes teaching them that it's *not* all right to ignore their homework, play ball in the house, leave their bike in the driveway, blast the music anywhere in or out of the house, or turn to screen time whenever they want.

## When Parents Have Difficulty Saying No

Parents often feel bad about saying no to their children. There can be many reasons for this: not wanting to disappoint your child, wishing to avoid confrontations, wanting her to like you as a friend, or wanting to treat her as an equal. Perhaps you felt your parents never listened to you and you don't want your children to feel that way. Busy parents who feel guilty about not giving a child enough attention may find it especially hard to refuse her anything.

*Parents who try too hard to please their child every day find the results disappointing.* The child is likely to end up grumpy and unappreciative of all the times she was allowed to have her way. When you and others say no to her, your child may become furious. Any child may act this way from time to time, but problems arise when it becomes an everyday pattern. In an extreme case, a seven-year-old might demand to decide what car the family buys and throw a tantrum in the showroom. She has come to believe that her parents should accept her opinion and influence and cave in to her demands.

Parents want to help their children feel respected and important. So it's hard to know where to draw the line between respecting your child and overindulging her. Five- to eight-year-olds should be getting past self-centeredness. *A child whose parents inadvertently support her self-centeredness can easily develop a strong sense of entitlement, a lack of empathy for others, and a low respect for her parents' needs as well.* This makes her a much less likable person. And frequent *conflicts* over control with your child can damage her self-esteem.

Be sure to respect your own needs. Good parenting nurtures both the child's and parent's needs and development. Make sure you tell your child how you feel when she says or does something that bothers you. This helps her be more tuned in to the effects of her behavior on others. *As an example, tell your child that when you have to ask her (or anyone) to do something over and over, it makes you frustrated and tired, and it's hard to be happy with her and want to do things with her.* This is the necessary "positive selfishness" mentioned earlier. When there's a conflict, make sure you ask your child to do something very nice for you to get back on your good side. *Expressing your needs can help your child understand that other people have needs to consider.*

## What Your Child Can Do for the Family

Five- to eight-year-olds are old enough to do some chores that help the family. *Although you may feel your children shouldn't have household responsibilities, kids who help out at home find it easier to comply with all the "have-tos" at school.* There are many benefits to having children share the household work.

• Doing chores together builds the spirit of "family," showing kids that everyone has to do his part.

• *Teaching children to do chores teaches them their parents' standards and work ethic.* We don't want our children to do tasks halfheartedly. School-age children who are resistant to doing chores often won't try their best at homework, sports, projects etc.

• Doing chores helps kids learn patience and perseverance. You'll see the results when your child readily accepts the structure and demands of school.

• Chores help children realize that ordinary and even tedious tasks are part of life. Then they'll appreciate the activities that are fun and amusing.

*It's best for five- to eight-year-olds to have chores they do seven days a week, so they don't argue and negotiate every Monday after a weekend break. One to three regular jobs a day, about five minutes each, is reasonable.* Teach your kids the jobs and try to do yours at the same time. They can do such tasks as setting and clearing the table, rinsing dishes, and loading and unloading the dishwasher. They can empty wastebaskets, sort recycling, put out garbage bins, and help with laundry, sweeping, and vacuuming. Pet-care chores are useful and also teach compassion. (Cooking probably shouldn't count as a chore, because it's fun for kids.) *Don't have your children alternate any chore with siblings, because they will hassle each other and you about unfairness.* (For example, if they alternate setting the table, you'll hear: "It's not fair because yesterday we had pizza, so you didn't have to put out any forks.")

To decrease resistance, every month or two, have your kids look at your master list of chores. Offer them the chance to keep the ones they have, to trade jobs with their siblings, or to choose new ones. Doing something new makes chores less boring and allows them to learn new skills.

## Frustration with Getting Our Children to Do What We Ask

*Parents know it's essential, but getting our kids to do what we tell them to is often our major challenge.* Common requests such as getting ready for school, putting their things away, ending screen time, and doing homework are frequent sources of conflict. Our children's most common reactions are ignoring, negotiating, or arguing with us.

As mentioned earlier (see pp. 27-28), having set routines helps a lot, but children still want to do what they want and don't always listen to what we tell them to do – even if they know what's expected. And since there are so many things we need them to do, there's a natural conflict. *(It helps us to remember that everything we ask of them teaches good lifelong habits.)*

Parents' most common complaint is that they have to tell their children over and over, and even if a child says yes, she still may not do what you asked – at least not soon enough. Parents get frustrated and angry, and worry that their children will listen to them less and less as they get older. This is why some parents start offering rewards/bribes to get their kids to listen. (More

about this on p.36, and more about consequences on pp. 37-39.) Lots of parents end up yelling and threatening consequences. We may even add "ever" to the consequence, such as: "Then you're not ever going to another sleepover" or "you're not ever getting your Legos back." However, *it's an extremely rare parent who carries out the "ever" threat.* Since children soon learn that parents won't carry out that threat, it would be best not to use it. *We don't want our children to learn that we say things we don't mean.*

## Why Won't Our Kids Do What We Say?

Parents have to teach children why they can't do what they want when they want.

*Here are some things that affect whether children learn to listen to their parents by the kindergarten to third-grade age.*

• *Children are more likely to listen if they get advance notice and aren't expected to stop what they're doing immediately to do what we say.* This is why routines are so helpful, but even with routines, parents

should give kids a few minutes' notice – even joining them in what they're doing to help bring their activity to an end or a temporary stop. When we ask our kids to do something, we should (silently) tell ourselves the reason. If it's just because we thought of it at the moment, that may not be a good enough reason to expect them to do it right now. For example: "Please put away the puzzles I just noticed on the coffee table."

Children from five to eight years old get involved in activities and find it hard to stop just because we suddenly realized we wanted them to do a task. Parents can work out a system where, along with their child, they make a **list of the things that don't have to be done immediately but do have to be done before dinner, before bed, etc.** Discuss this plan with your child so he knows that you will let him accumulate all your requests, as long as he does them by the agreed-upon deadline, such as dinner or bedtime.

• *Children aren't likely to listen to us if we tell them over and over.* They learn that they don't have to listen the first five or ten times, until there is fury in our voices or big consequences about to start. If you want your child to listen the first time (or the second), you should make sure you use a firm and no-nonsense tone, and *start the consequence after the first reminder – before you're really angry and before your child has learned to ignore you the first five or more times.* Telling them over and over also makes children feel nagged and irritated.

• *Children won't listen if they don't accept why we're making the request.* They may not believe it's important or necessary to do it now. (e.g., coming in to eat when you call them, putting their shoes away, or brushing their teeth). At more relaxed times, you can mention some of your regular requests and *see how well they can explain why you ask that of them* (e.g., how does it help them now and in the future, and how does it help the family?). Don't settle for one brief, superficial answer, or for the always popular "I don't know."

• *Children won't listen as well if we always tell them all the necessary steps rather than expecting them to remember the details.* For example, you say, "Remember, your job every night this month is to set the table. I want you to get the forks, knives, spoons, plates..."

or, "You've left all the scraps from your project on the kitchen table. Please get the garbage can from the hall and put all the scraps in it. Then put the scissors and the markers away in the kitchen desk drawer..." **When parents act like they are their child's memory bank, children end up taking no responsibility for remembering the steps.** It's better to say, "When it's time to set the table, what do you need to ask me so you'll know what to set the table with?" And regarding cleanup of scraps, it's better to say, "There are still things there that aren't OK to leave out."

As mentioned earlier, *these are also thought-provoking questions that encourage children to be better thinkers.* Here are some more examples: How can you find out what the weather is supposed to be like today (so he'll pick appropriate clothes)? Where else could it be (when your child asks you to find a misplaced item)? What would have been a better thing for that child to do (when another child is misbehaving)? What bothers me about what just happened (when you're unhappy about a situation)?

• *Children learn to listen if we don't back down when we ask them to do something.* Too many kids have learned that when they test the limit by disagreeing or ignoring, their parents give in. For example, you tell your child he has five minutes until he has to go to bed or take a shower or pick up toys, and he says, "No, I want ten minutes." *If your tendency has been to say yes to the ten minutes,* followed by, "But when the ten minutes are up, I expect you to listen to me," children *won't* expect to listen to you.

• *Children test our limits to see if we mean it and whether we'll cave in*. Giving in completely or giving him concessions make a child likely to negotiate with nearly everything we ask. These are situations where we can choose to **parent for the short term or the long term.** When we stop giving them concessions and help them understand the reasons for what we ask, our children will respect us more as the people in charge.

• *Children may not listen to us if we have very little time for them*. They may purposely be trying to get more time with us, which is called seeking "negative attention." All parents feel guilty on occasion for not giving their kids enough time. Kids need some predictable time when parents give them full and not half attention. They need you to do fun things with them as well as chores; to remember what's important to them and talk about it with them; and to spend time sharing some of your experiences and feelings and hearing about theirs. They also need not to be rushed too much. This is what we should strive for every week – not necessarily every day, but certainly **not only on vacations and holidays.**

• *Some children may not listen if they have inborn characteristics of extreme persistence, distractibility, or high activity levels*. Highly persistent children have a harder time stopping what they're saying or doing. Distractible children have difficulty completing what we ask them to do. Very active children may not be able to control their behavior enough to comply well. (See pp. 43-44 for suggestions on how to guide those children.) If your strategies and those of your child's teacher have not helped enough, ask your pediatrician for advice and/or for a referral to a specific type of professional who can help.

## Guiding Our Children to Want to Please Us

Parenting requires teaching our beliefs, values, and standards to our kids. That's very difficult, but *exceptionally* rewarding. A common example is getting our kids to put away their things, which, as expected, takes much teaching. By elementary-school age, everyone in the family should be expected to clean up after themselves daily. We want children to learn that when they do their part, we have time to spend with them because we didn't have to tell them over and over or threaten consequences. *Children feel good emotionally and even physiologically when we smile, praise them, hug them, and have time to be with them. That builds their desire to do what we ask.*

Children **want to please us** if our demands are reasonable, justifiable, age-appropriate, and consistent. *They don't want to please us if our demands don't meet those criteria*. They feel good if we're happy, affectionate, and available to them, which lets them know how pleased we are. *But if there is no end to our demands, they may feel that no matter what they do, they'll never be done or never be able to please us.* Even children who are internally driven to do all that we ask may start ignoring our pressure. This happens frequently in families where parents keep giving the kids more and more jobs and/or in families where parents pressure children for accomplishments or tell them, "I just want you to do your best." Although in the latter case those parents say they're just trying to motivate their kids to try harder, their children may feel like they're being asked to do the impossible, because they know a person can always do better.

*It's valuable for parents to spend time assisting in their child's classroom – even just monthly – and at the child's other activities. This way we know what the demands are on them, in terms of how their teachers run the class, what skills are expected, and how they're doing.* Children feel much closer to us when we can relate to what is going on in their lives and help them with expectations and stresses. They're more likely to respect us and want to please us when they feel we understand their world, and because our advice makes better sense when it is well informed.

Children are more receptive to us when they want to please us. As they learn that they please us with small things such as putting their things away and going to bed on time, and bigger things such as doing what they're

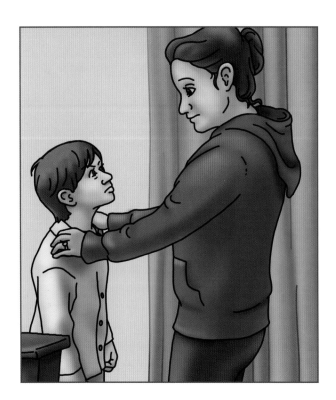

capable of without demanding our help and doing good jobs rather than half-jobs, they develop a valuable belief system. If we have good values and they want to please us (as most children do), our teaching is the foundation for the person they become. If we show good values, kids learn them: being hardworking, friendly, considerate of others, honest, healthy, good thinkers, etc.

Encouraging them to want to please us helps youngsters who just want to do what they want evolve into young adults who know how and why to behave, who know who they are and what they believe, who learn and accomplish things, and who know how to get along with others, including how to understand people and how to respond to them.

### Don't Pay Your Child to Listen to You

Some parents believe they have to give children material rewards for listening – marbles in a jar, a sticker or a check mark on a chart with a material reward as the end goal. That means we haven't succeeded in teaching them that there are many things everyone has to do, and that it's our job to guide them. *It means the parent-child relationship is missing key ingredients: the child's acceptance of our role and her desire to please us.* Some

parents have come to believe it's right or reasonable to bribe children to do what we say because it's expedient. But this approach leads children to want more things, then more expensive things, and then more frequently, *and* it makes children feel controlled and manipulated, knowing they'll get the material reward only if they do what you say. Those parents are also likely to threaten to take away a prized possession if their kids don't continue to listen. This approach causes a lot of anger for kids. The antidote is making sure your child wants to please you, understands your job as a parent, and accepts the reasons for your request.

### Don't Bargain or Make Deals with Your Child

*Sometimes a child will respond to our request, "I'll only do that if you do this."* For example, you ask him to straighten his room and he says he'll only do it if you clean up the toys in the family room that you've been asking him to pick up since yesterday. Children who respond that way have often heard us say something similar, such as: "I'll only play soccer with you if you unload the dishwasher." (*It would be better to refer to household expectations and say, "We play after we do our jobs."*) We may be unaware that we're making deals that imply "I will only do this for you if I get something from you" so that it's not surprising that our children use this tactic on us. This irritates parents and feels like an unfriendly power grab, which isn't what we want our relationship to our children to be.

It's better to make sure your child knows why you want him to do what you ask, and that when it's done well in a reasonable amount of time, you'll be pleased and would love to spend time with him. Let him know that while he's doing the task, you'll be doing one too. If he doesn't do his task, tell him you're frustrated and disappointed that he hasn't done what he needs to and hasn't learned what you need to teach him, and what all parents need to teach their kids. And tell him that now you're too rushed to spend time with him.

If he tries to get you to do something for him in exchange for complying, tell him that it's not OK to bargain about cooperating. Remind him that grownups are in charge. As a consequence, aside from missing out on time with you, he might have to do more tasks. *However, you can only fix this behavior in your child if you don't model it in the first place.*

## Consequences

Consequences teach your child to do what she should without your having to tell her over and over. They teach her to think twice before she repeats the misbehavior. Of course, most parents wish they didn't have to punish their children – *the rule-enforcement part of parenting is certainly not what many of us enjoy in child-rearing, but it's necessary.* It's an extremely rare child who can be raised well without consequences.

*Parents need more consequences to use than just the current favorites of time-out and taking things or privileges away.* Too few consequences means that children can anticipate what the punishment will be and can act like these consequences don't bother them (e.g., "go ahead and take all my Legos. I don't care") – maybe convincing us that we have no meaningful consequences. *To parent effectively, we need at least five consequences so our children can't anticipate what the punishment might be.*

### New Consequences
### Practicing better behavior

Most commonly, when children do things they shouldn't, parents tell them not to do that again: "Stop throwing the ball in the house. I've told you not to do that. Now, don't do it again. Do you understand?" or, "I won't let you do that" while the child is doing that. *What works better than telling him what not to do is getting him to practice doing what he should do, typically three times in a row.* With throwing the ball inside, help him figure out several *acceptable* outside locations and have him take the ball and throw it there several times. You can have him figure out what *he* can say to himself to remind himself not to throw it inside.

*There are many uses for the consequence of practicing better behavior.* Practicing is a much faster, more effective way for children to learn to behave better – to internalize better behavior. If your child won't cooper-

ate, use time-out (as described on p. 38), and after time-out, he still needs to practice the better behavior. Here are some examples.

- **When children are rude** (saying things like, "I know what I want to do and what I don't want to do. You don't," or, "You pick it up!" or, "Get me my food!") we can have them figure out the more diplomatic, respectful way to say what they want to say, and then say it. If what they practice saying is acceptable to us, then we should have them say it several more times so this *better behavior becomes internalized.* If your child seems too young to be able to find a kinder way to talk to you, or is unwilling to, you can tell him what to say and have him practice it three times in a row. Listen to the words and the tone your child uses. We shouldn't accept silly or mocking voices. *Nor should we accept sarcasm or use it with our kids.* (Of course, he and you might conclude that there's no kind way to say what he wanted to, so it's best for him to tell himself not to say it at all.)

- **When children leave their things out** (like clothes, school books and papers, food wrappers and plates), you can ask a thought-provoking question like, "What do you still need to do in this room?" and then have the child put the things away. If you then have him take the things back out and do it twice more, he'll remember better in the future, because anyone would want to avoid the tedium of this repetition.

- **When children ignore you**, tell them that for the next 15 (or 30) minutes, you'll be calling their name a lot, and each time, they need to say, "What, Mom?" or "What, Dad?" Explain that you'll let them know whether they have to do something you ask or just answer you. *Call their names about every two minutes.* You may need to repeat this consequence a few times in the next few days. This is memorably annoying for young children and makes it more likely that they will stop ignoring you.

- **When children aren't making an effort to put away their toys**, you can set a timer for a few minutes and let them know if the toys aren't cleaned up by then, that means they need a lot more practice, so *you'll have to* make another mess for them to clean up. Then follow through if needed.

### Wasted time

Children need to know that there will be a consequence when they have wasted a lot of our time by not doing what we asked. *If you have to tell your child over and over and/or end up doing a lot of the job yourself, then that has used up a lot of your time.*

For your five- and six-year-olds, and those older ones who still love to help with our chores, tell them that because so much of your time has been wasted, you're behind in your chores. *You won't be able to do something special you had wanted to do with them later that day* – even if they didn't know about it – such as baking, playing a board game, or doing a special project together. For the seven- and eight-year-olds who no longer love to help us with our chores, tell them, "So much of my time has been wasted that I'm behind with my tasks. Now so you'll have to do my next job" (or two). Pick something that takes at least 15 minutes and is pretty tedious, such as weeding, cleaning out the silverware drawer, or sorting all the socks in the clean laundry.

### Empathy consequence

*It's useful for children to understand how to get back on the good side of someone they've annoyed.* When you're really frustrated, disappointed, or angry with your child because of her behavior, have her sit at the table and ask her to figure out what you're thinking (or feeling) about her right now and why. (Make sure you haven't already told her the answer.) Don't accept a one-word answer, such as "bad, sad, mad." *Have her "think harder."* After a few weeks of practice, when she gets used to answering this question, have her tell you two things you're thinking or feeling about her and why. *Or for a more impactful empathy consequence*, you can tell her what you're feeling about her and then tell her that she needs to do something very nice for you to get back on your good side. Have her think of three things and let her know whether they would make you happy with her. If none of them do, see if she can figure out why. Make sure she comes up with more ideas, such as bringing you your favorite beverage or giving you a foot or hand massage. If she's not cooperating, let her know you're still not happy with her. Limit your smiles, attention, and conversation with her until she finds a way to get back on your good side. (Also, read the guidance article "Teaching Empathy to Your Child" by this author on the www.PerfectingParentingPress.com website.) *Boring and tedious consequences are usually memorable and therefore effective for children without the negative effects of the now-discredited consequences of pain, fear, and humiliation.*

## Improved Consequences
### Time-out

Time-out is usually useful for children up to about eight years. *It allows parents to make the point that their child's behavior is so unacceptable (uncivilized, unsocialized) that he needs to be away from the rest of the family.* Time-out should be in the child's bedroom with the door shut so he can't see or hear the rest of the family. *It's best not to use other time-out spots around the house.* When we use these "naughty spots," our children usually do annoying things like moving along the floor or getting on and off the chair, often making noise or calling out to us. Then we are forced to engage with them – which frustrates us more and defeats the purpose of *no involvement during time-out.*

Consider whether you need to remove some things from your child's room if he needs a lot of time-outs. Many five- to eight-year-olds can amuse themselves with their toys, books etc., so time-out can lose its impact as a consequence. If that's a problem, you might choose a less interesting place, like *your* bedroom, a guest room, or the laundry room. Continue to use one minute per year of age for the time-out. And consider assigning him a thought-provoking question or two for him to ponder during time-out, like, "What bothered me (the parent) about what you did? What's a better way the next time I ask you to...?" and expect an answer at the end of the time-out. If he's old enough, have him write a paragraph explaining to you why he misbehaved and what he should have done instead. *This gets the child to think about what he did while he is in time-out – something parents wish their kids would do, but we all know that they don't – unless they have an assignment!* You can also get him to practice the better behavior after time-out.

## Taking things or privileges away from children

This is a reasonable consequence *as long as it's not the only one you use with your child.* If we try to control our kids' behavior exclusively by threatening to take away their favorite item or activities, we make them angrier at us and less able to accept our punishment.

A consequence should make sense and teach our children something that makes them more willing to behave. It's effective to take things away as a consequence when kids leave their possessions outside, hurt a sibling with a toy, take others' things, or destroy someone's property, including ours. Taking away dessert from a child who hasn't eaten enough of a healthy dinner or taking a toy away from a child who has ignored you over and over while playing with it makes sense to us and to our children. Telling our children they can't go to the movies or any other planned outing because of their difficult behavior is reasonable too, as long as the person the child stays home with makes the time less than enjoyable. But when we threaten to take away something of extreme importance to them, such as their electronic devices, children are often furious. They feel *forced* to give in to us. Then they want to retaliate in some way – or just scream at us in rage.

*Some parents use this threat over and over to control their child's behavior: "If you don't do what I said, I'm taking away your (video games, tablet etc.)"* This can lead to lots of hostility between kids and parents. It does not help a child learn to behave better when she does so only to keep a prized possession from being taken away. The children who get most angry about this are the ones who spend too much time with their devices, including sneaking more time than they're allowed. If this is a problem in your home, use this opportunity to set realistic limits on their use of electronic devices, so they don't continue their "addiction." *For kindergartners to third-graders, an hour a day of recreational screen time, including TV time, should be the maximum on weekdays.* Since this can cause your child to rush through her homework, many parents try to limit recreational screen time to weekends, when two hours a day should be the maximum. *If you want to allow recreational screen time daily, try allowing it*

*before homework.* See if your child does better knowing the screen time is now up for the day. Then there would be less reason to rush through homework. Screen time is a very different, easily addicting type of play activity. Try allowing all the weekend screen time early in the day, so when it's done your child can focus on finding other ways to enjoy herself. It's very hard for children to end their screen time, which to them means stopping the endless entertaining and interactive options *and returning to the world of parental control.*

## When Consequences Cause Children to Spiral Out of Control

*Some children tend to become furious when they hear what their consequence will be, no matter what it is.* Parents then have to decide whether their child is trying to get them to give up on the consequence or whether their child's view of the situation (as seen through his self-talk) is so one-sided that he is now completely out of control.

If you think it's the former, you need to be firm, clear, and confident about the consequence rather than being afraid of his anger. If you think it's the latter, you can try empathy – "Things are hard now. We'll wait a little while to do the consequence" – changing the narrative to something more comforting like suggesting he read or go to his room for a while, or offering a hug to calm him

down. **And use your best tactic to calm yourself down.** When your child calms down, you'll want to work with him on why parents have consequences, why his grand-parents had consequences for you, and why you wanted him to do what you first asked. Talking to him about why he refused and seeing his perspective can be useful, **though he still needs the consequence.** Make sure you're helping him with his self-talk (see p. 41).

### Children's Strong Reactions to Our Becoming More Confident Parents

As we make the changes that help put us in charge and **minimize the "equal say democracy" in our homes, children initially become quite angry.** We can help them cope with their strong feelings and understand why we're making changes, what's going on inside of them, and what they can do about it.

With five- to eight-year-olds, we certainly want to explain the changes, telling them what we'll be doing differently and why. Without an explanation, they will likely be surprised, confused, and very resistant, and may shut down with us. **Parents should talk to each of their kindergarten to third-grade kids separately, and say:** "For a long time, we've let you decide things

that parents should decide, like what restaurant we're going to or what errand we're going to do next, or what we're having for dinner.* Kids your age aren't old enough or experienced enough to decide a lot of things. When we've taken charge and decided things, you've gotten so angry that we have started to realize we've let you have your way too often. From now on, we're going to be telling you the rules and why we have the rules. It will take a while for you to get used to the new rules, but soon they'll make sense to you." *(Parents should reread the children's story in this book to themselves to help them explain these changes to their child.)*

*As we initiate changes that reduce that equal-ity between our children and us, and as we work on being clear and confident in our reasons, we should also look at what our child is experiencing. Children benefit from knowing we understand their perspec-tive.* For example, let's say it's time for your child to stop playing and to set the table for dinner. You give her a few minutes' warning and let her know what's being served so she can figure out what silverware is needed – but she still doesn't stop playing. When you remind her again, she tells you that she needs some time, *or* she ignores you *or* she complains that you're being unfair, etc. To become a respected parent, **you have to tell yourself the reasons** you asked **this** of her **now.** But it's also true that your child is frustrated because it's unacceptable to you that she wants to keep playing. You need to socialize her – to train her – to accept that in your family and in society, people have tasks they have to do despite their personal wishes at the moment. Parents want to help our children to accept these responsibilities without becoming angry.

*So, when she wants more time, ignores, or complains, it can help to say, "Of course you don't want to stop playing. You're enjoying what you're doing.* But there's a routine, just like in school when the teachers tell you it's time to do the next thing. It's frustrating and it can make kids angry." You can also say, "I feel that way many times a day – even in the evening when I see it's 10 o'clock and I don't want to stop what I'm doing. So I tell myself I have to stop even if I don't want to, so I can get enough sleep and won't be exhausted tomorrow."

You can recommend that your child use self-talk or

inner dialogue to calm herself: "I think it can help if you tell yourself, 'Even if I don't want to, I have to stop what I'm doing now. Mom made my favorite dinner and I want to tell Mom and Dad about my school science project. I can play some more after dinner.' "

Sometimes kids are so frustrated by our requests that they say or do something unacceptable that makes us furious. They may scream that we're the meanest, worst parents in the world, that they're going to live with Grandma and Grandpa, that this is "the worst day of my life," or that *we* should leave the family. They may threaten to destroy something of ours, and even do it. *We can help them understand why they said or did what they did and explain what comes next.* For example: As soon as their anger cools a little, we can say, "I think (not "I know") the reason you said *that* is because you were so mad when I told you to clean up your room that you couldn't remember why I asked you to do it, or how many times I reminded you in the last two days and how many times you promised to do it. You probably just thought, 'Mom is horrible – I hate her – she never lets me do what I want – everything has to be her way.' " You can explain that when she tells herself these things, it makes her even more upset. As a consequence, tell her: "Since you know what you did isn't OK, take some time at the table and work on telling yourself why I told you to clean up your room. When you remember the reasons, tell me what they are. Then we'll figure out how you can make up for what you said to me and when you really will clean up your room."

Sometimes our kids will argue or get more angry about this or any consequence. *We don't want to debate our consequences with our children as if we both had equal say. We need to say, "This – and nothing else – is what I expect of you."* We don't want to model ignoring. Instead, give a shrug and a look that says, "I'm not debating this." If your child walks away, ignores, says something ruder, or has a tantrum, repeat: "This – and nothing else – is what I expect of you." After a while, a child will seek out her parents. When she does, your consequence still stands, and you should add to it. One way to do that is to interrupt her with repeated requests over the next few hours. *Tell her why you're doing that and help her practice what she can tell herself so she can accept the interruptions rather than telling herself*

*the wrong things, which make her resistant.* We don't want our kids believing they can walk away from our request and all will be well.

## Teaching Our Kids Good Self-Talk

You can use recent examples of when you felt very mad and started saying things to yourself that made you even madder, until you realized that was a bad idea: "That man in line ahead of me is taking forever. Why can't he find his credit card? He's sure wasting my time." Explain that you made yourself think about why the man might have been slow, and how that calmed you down. ("Maybe he had a hard day and is too tired to think clearly.") Describe the whole incident so your child knows grownups can have the same problems and that they're not easy for us either.

You can teach him to tell himself the reasons you are having him stop playing now – "we have to clean up before our friends come over for dinner" – *so he can see someone else's perspective and bring this balancing thought into his poor self-talk so it becomes more rational and reasonable.* At another time, you can re-visit some recent examples of when he got angrier and angrier. You can probably guess some things he said to himself to make him more furious (such as "Mom thinks I'm her slave" – "Dad doesn't care what I think or how I feel") and help him figure out what he could say to himself to get on the right track in his self-talk. (Of course, self-talk can also be used for other difficult feelings, such as sadness and anxiety.)

## How to Determine if Your Handling of the Incident Went Well

*Ask yourself what your child learned at the end of the incident.* Usually, we want our children to learn these things:

- Why we wanted her to do what we said.

- We meant what we said and didn't give in.

- After she did what we expected, we were satisfied and happy with her.

We don't want the incident to *end* in the child's tantrum or ours, or with us just giving in. And we don't want her to believe that we have no effective consequences – that she just gets her way. Here's an example of a poor outcome: The parent asks the six-year-old to clean up her toys. After 20 minutes of arguing and negotiating, the parent has picked up 90% of the toys and the child has picked up the remaining few. *The child has learned that she can get her parent to do almost the whole job – not what we want to teach.*

Your child gained something valuable if she learned that: you had good reasons for what you asked, you were confident in your expectations, and you gave no concessions. That's what you want. Child-rearing is filled with our requests, resistance from our kids in many different forms, lots of skirmishes, and hopefully many useful outcomes.

## What Goals Should We Have for Our Children?

Kids need to know that it's our job to teach them everything six-year-olds (or seven-year-olds, etc.) need to know about how to behave – even when we're busy, tired, or sick. *It's worthwhile for them to know that the things we teach them will make their life better.* The things we teach them include learning how to take care of themselves, getting jobs done, being friendly to others, handling difficult feelings, being honest, not giving up easily when something is hard, getting enough sleep and exercise, and eating healthy foods.

*Parents should periodically discuss with each other their big goals for their children.* These include being responsible, considerate, hard-working, honest, friendly, and respectful, living a healthy lifestyle, and becoming problem-solvers. When parents agree on their goals for their children's future, they can work together on the harder part: what steps to take to help their children develop these important life skills.

There are many resources to help with the steps. Usually, your child's teachers can let you know when your child is having trouble in any of these areas. They see your child alongside many others of the same age, and often have years of experience with hundreds of children. Their advice can be a good starting point. You'll also want to do some research and reading about

these issues, using this and other books, articles, online resources, etc., and discuss them with your friends, family, pediatrician, and especially your spouse. Sometimes parents feel they've tried everything and nothing works – they're at their wits' end. If your child is still having significant difficulties that are causing him, you, and others problems, ask his teacher or pediatrician for a referral. Referrals might be made to mental-health, social-skills, learning, language, or motor-skills specialists.

## Working Together as Parenting Partners

*To help you be partners in parenting*, you and your spouse should have *private conversations* a few times each week about situations where the two of you had different approaches. Telling your spouse he or she is wrong in front of your children creates many problems. The insulted parent will feel undermined and disrespected. He or she may argue angrily with you or give up on parenting your child *when you're present*. In raising children, parents need to be partners.

Most parents react to their child's behavior quickly and without a lot of thought. *When you take the time to explain the reason for your parenting decision to your spouse after the kids are asleep, you are also clarifying your logic and reasoning to yourself.* These chats need to be like "show and tell," with each spouse first listening and then asking thoughtful questions to understand one another better.

*Parents should ask each other more about "why" so they can understand the thinking and goals behind each other's parenting actions.* This process is usually insightful and productive. After the couple understand each other's views, the debate can begin. This helps parents gain respect for each other's methods and learn from each other so they can develop a closer collaboration as partners, and perhaps incorporate some of the other's approach into their own. Frequent exchanges between parents also help each parent feel more confident about the way the other handles child-rearing issues.

This method can help parents avoid giving in, disagreeing or correcting each other in front of their children, or giving up and walking away. This enlightening and eventually enjoyable process helps bring

couples together, one situation at a time, until they reach greater understanding over the years. Eventually, the couple will come to better trust the intent behind their spouse's child-rearing actions, and they won't need these discussions as frequently.

**When parents fail to work together, their child may lose confidence in her parents' ability to set reasonable yet firm limits as well as to have appropriate consequences.** She may become increasingly challenging to raise and may begin to disrespect one or even both parents. It's obvious to a child when her parents disagree, insult, or undermine each other. A lot of family tension arises from parents' inability to agree and to respect each other's approach to child-rearing. Children need their parents to be sufficiently consistent with each other. Vocal disagreements between parents leave children aware that they can manipulate this weakness in their parents' gatekeeping. It also leaves them confused and angry. They may be afraid to ask about their deepest fear: "Are you going to get a divorce?"

Some parents need professional counseling to understand the effect their very different – and maybe even opposing – parenting styles and lack of respect for each other have on their child's behavior and personality, and to learn to work together better in guiding their children.

## Guiding Our More Difficult Kids

*Most people who have more than one child know that our children are often very different from each other.* One child may be much more compliant than the others. Another may be highly active, hardly able to stay still long enough to hear your requests. His energy level requires many more rules than other children need – including rules about risk-taking and property damage – as well as energy-burning activities and equipment, such as a trampoline. Another may be in his own world a lot – so focused on his own interests and thoughts that he has to be taught how to listen when someone talks to him. And another child can have a persistent or relentless personality and may keep debating, arguing, and asking till you're worn down.

## Here are some suggestions for those children:

• *For the active child who needs to use up energy, provide before-school opportunities such as running and kicking his soccer ball around a big space.* Join him as much as you can to model using up energy without the risk-taking, and tell him (or model for him) what to say to herself so he doesn't hurt himself or others, including you. Give him jobs that use energy, such as carrying laundry and taking out garbage cans.

• *The "in his own world" child needs time to be on his own, but he should be expected to interact at meals, in the car, with friends, on outings.* He shouldn't read when he's with others, and has to be taught to pull himself out of his concentration when others talk to him. Teach him what to say to himself, such as: "Someone is talking to me; I have to answer him." (Of course, you would have had his hearing checked already, and you should look for any patterns that raise concern, including not understanding what's said to him or having very little to say.)

• *The persistent, relentless child insists on what he wants and seems to have an unending battery life.* Teach him that you don't like it when anyone keeps talking and talking because you have other things you need to think about. If telling him you can't listen anymore isn't enough, have him go to his room. Be sure he doesn't expect you to keep talking to him when he misbehaves.

Instead, develop non-verbal signals such as a shrug to use with him so you don't model ignoring. Even if he's a people person who craves interaction or an audience or talks till he gets his way, your job is to make sure his behavior is acceptable to society.

## Children's More Challenging Behaviors

### When homework is a hassle

Many children resist doing homework. Homework is usually given beginning in first grade, usually starting at about 15 minutes a night and increasing grade by grade. More than a half to one hour a night for first through third grade would be too much. In this case, parents may choose to talk to the teacher or, if necessary, the principal.

Children in first and second grade typically do homework with a parent, usually at the kitchen table. By third grade, most children have more self-discipline and can benefit from the independence of working at a desk in their room. Parents, however, still need to do some checking on their child and on her work. *They should discuss with the teacher how much help to give.*

Many children (and even parents) feel homework is an intrusion into their after-school time. It can be. So it's useful to parents to learn to accept that the school regards homework as valuable. *We are really the middlemen between the teachers and children when it comes to homework, and need to have the right attitude, one that will work for our kids*. Routines for homework are helpful. Children should not be overloaded with after-school activities. They need time for a snack and free play, and should have a goal of getting homework done by dinner, with more freedom after dinner. After-school programs often have staff who will help supervise the homework. Then parents can do a briefer homework check in the evenings and do some homework – if possible – with their kids on the weekends. For many children, it's a good idea to help them decide what homework to do first and what you should be "on standby" to assist with. Some do better doing the harder parts first and others need the opposite. Some children will need small breaks if there's lots of homework.

*If you see mistakes and/or sloppy work in your* child's finished homework, discuss with the teacher what you should do. It is likely disheartening and even infuriating to a child if you point out and make her fix every error. You could tell her that you see about X number of places that need a second look from her. Then ask her how many of those she wants to take a look at. Putting this control in her hands can help a lot when you're delivering bad news. You don't want her to feel you're fine with mistakes and sloppiness, but you also don't want to correct her homework so extensively that she hates doing homework and the teacher can't see where she needs help. *If you don't point out more mistakes than they can handle, many kids will respond over time by being willing to correct more and more of them.*

### When our children won't apologize – to anyone

Many children don't want to say they're sorry when they've done something they shouldn't have. Some children go to great lengths to avoid apologizing, and even accept consequences instead. When children refuse to apologize, adults get concerned that their youngsters don't feel remorse. Does our child have no conscience or empathy? Or worse, is he a sociopath? A future criminal? We wonder what to do.

Parents and teachers used to teach children from the

earliest ages to say "I'm sorry" for any mishap, accidental or deliberate. Then, about 15 years ago, a theory took hold in preschools. It discouraged adults from insisting that a child say "I'm sorry" if he really isn't. An insincere apology, this theory holds, is of no real value. Since then, many children have not developed what should be an automatic habit of saying "I'm sorry." Instead, these children view apologizing as some sort of horrible admission of guilt, a surrender, or a humiliation, and refuse to do it. The theory held that children would eventually learn to understand that they had hurt someone, and would *sincerely* feel sorry and decide to apologize. That hasn't happened.

*Just as young children should start saying "thank you" even if they won't learn to be truly appreciative for many years, they should also be taught to say "I'm sorry" – for emotional and physical hurts, accidental or purposeful.* When young children learn to say they're sorry, they come to realize they shouldn't have done what they did or should be regretful even if it was an accident, and most learn, over time, to be sincerely sorry and willing to accept blame. To help your child become comfortable with apologizing, ask him why he believes he doesn't need to *and* tell him why you *now* think apologizing is an important courtesy. Help him explore how he feels when he apologizes. Try to relate to his perspective so he knows that you're aware of how hard this will be. *If your child doesn't believe in apologizing, explain what a negative impression people get of someone who won't say he's sorry.* Tell him that others will think he doesn't regret what he did and that he only cares about himself, and that most people don't want to be around that kind of person or have their children be with them. Make sure he knows that people do like others better if they apologize when they upset someone. Lots of children don't know that.

Tell your child that apologizing (such as, "I'm sorry" or "I didn't mean to do that") doesn't automatically say that you did something terrible or horrible. Remind him that he should apologize for things like getting ahead of someone in line, stepping on someone's foot, or saying something that hurt someone's feelings. Expect him to do that with family as well.

You want your kids to see you being considerate. So when you do something that bothers someone, *make sure you apologize.* Then your child sees how automatic it is. (Remember, most people apologize to others many times in a typical day – it's viewed as basic kind behavior.)

### When our children lie to us

Very young children tend to be forthright – they surprise us by telling us what happened even though they're "telling on" themselves. But by age four, most children start covering up the truth when they realize it could them them into trouble. When we sound accusatory by saying, for example, "Did you take your brother's yo-yo?" it's natural for most kids to deny it. When parents use this approach, children will continue to deny their actions. In their frustration, parents say things to their child such as, "You're lying." "Just tell me the truth." "I won't be mad if you're just honest with me." "Now you're getting a consequence for lying." Children who hear that they are being labeled liars may feel that's how they're seen, so why not keep lying?

*If we know that our child took the yo-yo, it's better to skip the accusation and say,* "It's not OK to do that. Let's figure out why you did it. Give it back to your brother, and let's see how you can make it up to him." If you can skip the *"did you do that?"* part, children are less likely to deny the misdeed. When we aren't sure, we can say, "Here's what I know so far. Here's what the person who did it would need to do to make up for that. So tell me everything you know about what happened and we'll go from there." Children are more likely to tell the truth if they know what their punishment will be and if they know the parent will calmly hear the whole story. Decreasing the heat and giving the situation calm attention is most effective. Of course, this can't be done every time, because it's time-consuming.

There are also other common situations in which kids are driven to lie because of the way parents ask the question. Questions like these can cause a child to lie: Did you brush your teeth? Did you clean your room? Do you have any homework? Did you finish your homework? *Asking the questions this way makes it too convenient for children to take the easy way out.* We don't want to make it easy for our children to lie to us, or

make them to feel we're easy to fool and try to get away with it as much as possible.

You can avoid this problem by phrasing your question differently, such as, "Have you had a chance to brush your teeth yet?" "Please look over your planner to see if you have any homework." Then check frequently; i.e., go to her room after you've asked if she's **had a chance** to clean it yet, rather than just calling out, "Did you clean up your room yet?" Children will find it easier to be truthful this way.

For some children, lying is a much bigger issue. It's done to try to get away with misdeeds, such as stealing a toy or money from a friend's house and claiming the friend gave it to her. Another type of lie is making up a story, such as the description of your family's amazing vacation (that never happened). There are many possible reasons for both kinds of troubling behavior. These include believing that others are treated better, feeling she lags behind her peers or sibs in many ways, having trouble resisting temptation, and acting out in response to major stresses in the family, such as parents traveling a lot for work, or a divorce.

If you think your child is having these problems, check in with the teacher and parents who spend time with your child to see if they've noticed her doing things she shouldn't. *Make sure your child feels good about herself in enough ways that she doesn't have to act out*

*by doing things she shouldn't and then cover them up by lying, or making up stories to try to impress people.* Take a close look at how she sees herself. She may need – at the least – regular one-on-one time with you so she can feel more valued. And be sure to spend time with your child in which you're not pressuring her to do better and better. That approach makes many kids feel inadequate. Don't forget to tell your child stories about what happened during a time when you lied as a child. If you need more help, talk to your child's teacher, her school counselor, her pediatrician, or a mental-health professional.

## Conclusion

*This book guides you through one of the biggest challenges that parents face raising kindergartners through third-graders: when a child demands to be his own boss.* We don't want our children to believe they have the right to make most of the decisions in the family and become furious when they can't. *Children need us to be reasonable, thoughtful, clear, and confident in our parenting.* They need us to establish routines and predictability, to be consistent enough so we gain their respect, and be willing to explain why we ask of them what we do. We want them to be informed and accepting about the decisions we make as parents, to be aware and empathetic about others' views, and to be better thinkers as they grow. As our kindergarten to third-grade children learn that we have good reasons behind what we say and that we will hear their opinions but not necessarily change ours, they are likely to develop expectations and values that will make their lives satisfying and successful. This is all about using today's best parenting approaches.

*When you put the advice in this book into practice, take it a piece at a time. It's not easy, but the results will be worth it.* It's important to your family that you help your elementary school children learn why they shouldn't and can't be the boss. This process will help in your parenting goals: to have an enjoyable, respectful, and satisfying family life where everyone is doing his or her job as a cooperative and considerate member of the family and of the community, now and in the future.

B. ANNYE ROTHENBERG, Ph.D., *author*, has been a child/parent psychologist and a specialist in child rearing and development of children from babies through age 10 for more than 25 years. Her parenting psychology practice is in Redwood City, CA. She is known for her home and school visits that enable her to understand the children and their parents more fully and provide very targeted guidance. Dr. Rothenberg is a frequent speaker to parent groups. She is also an adjunct clinical assistant professor of pediatrics at Stanford University School of Medicine and consults to pediatricians and teachers. She was the founder/director of the Child Rearing parenting program in Palo Alto, CA, and is the author of the award-winning book *Parentmaking* (Banster Press, 1982, 1995) and other parent education books for parenting guidance professionals. Dr. Rothenberg is the author of all the books in the award-winning series for preschoolers, kindergartners, and their parents: *Mommy and Daddy Are Always Supposed To Say Yes … Aren't They?* (2007), *Why Do I Have To?* (2008), *I Like To Eat Treats* (2009), *I Don't Want To Go To The Toilet* (2011), *I Want To Make Friends* (2012) and *I'm Getting Ready For Kindergarten* (2013). *Why Can't I Be The Boss Of Me* is the **first** in her new kindergarten to third grade series. She is the mother of one grown-up son.

BONNIE BRIGHT, *illustrator,* has been a professional illustrator of children's books for 15 years. She also illustrates and animates digital books, and was previously an art director, game artist and animator during a 15-year educational computer game career. She has done 3-D artwork and animation for major movie web sites, such as *Shrek* and *Kung Fu Panda*. Her illustrated books include *I Want To Make Friends*, *I'm Getting Ready For Kindergarten*, *The Tangle Tower, Surf Angel*, and *I Love You All The Time*. She is married, has two daughters, and lives in San Diego, CA. Her web site is *www.brightillustration.com*

## ACKNOWLEDGEMENTS

The author is extremely grateful to *SuAnn and Kevin Kiser* for their continuing and outstanding critiques and collaboration on the children's story and to *Caroline Grannan* for her thorough and excellent editing of the parents' manual. *Cathleen O'Brien* has again shown her terrific creativity and talent in the book design she has created. *Bonnie Bright's* work as an illustrator has been the best.

Many people were willing to spend time providing thoughtful suggestions and reviews of this manuscript. We are most grateful for the time and efforts of *Pauline Warren, M.A., LMFT, Lower School Counslor (K to 3rd grade) at the Harker School,* San Jose, CA, and to the following San Francisco Bay Area parents of elementary school children: *Kim O'Keefe Beck, Tonya Kaufman, Lama and Ramez Nachman, Christine Neer and Howard Jones*, and *Evelyn Wildgans.*

⭐ *Dr. Rothenberg's "Why Can't I Be the Boss of Me" book was an eye opener for me. Finding a happy medium where parents can empower their children to be independent and make age appropriate choices without spoiling them on one hand or micromanaging them on the other hand is key to raising happy well-adjusted kids. I found the examples in the parents handbook extremely helpful in understanding that balance and in applying them to my own situation. I strongly recommend this book for parents with kids especially in grades K-3.*
    — **Lama Nachman, mother of a 7 year old boy and Research Scientist, San Francisco, CA**

⭐ *This book by Dr. Rothenberg does an excellent job of guiding parents and children about this difficult issue of who is the "boss" in the family. She explains the "why" and "how" so parents learn the ways to resolve these difficulties. The story for children helps them understand why the parents have to lead. The book is a valuable resource. I recommend it for parents and teachers as well as for pediatricians, child psychologists and psychiatrists. It helps professionals explain their reasoning behind the advice they give as well as the specifics of the advice.*
    — **Elizabeth A. Herb, M.D.; Child Psychiatrist, Palo Alto, CA, and Clinical Associate Professor Emerita, Dept. of Psychiatry, Stanford University School of Medicine.**

# Be sure to read Dr. Annye Rothenberg's other *all-in-one* books
### *for preschoolers, kindergartners, and their parents*

## Mommy And Daddy Are Always Supposed To Say Yes...Aren't They?

A STORY FOR CHILDREN— Alex insists that his parents should always let him have what he wants. In this story, he begins to see things differently and learns that even when Mom and Dad say no, they still love him ... a lot.   INCLUDES A PARENT MANUAL—*Why don't children get the message about who's the parent?* How to give your child just enough say. What if they want more? How do you deal realistically with the differences between your parenting and your spouse's?

## Why Do I Have To?

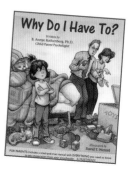

A STORY FOR CHILDREN—Sophie wonders why there are so many rules and why her parents want her to follow them. This story teaches the answers.   INCLUDES A PARENT MANUAL—Explains how preschoolers think, how to make it easier for your children to do what you ask, and the better and most effective consequences. *This manual clears up much of the conflicting advice that parents hear.*

## I Like To Eat Treats

A STORY FOR CHILDREN—Jack wants to eat whatever he wants. His parents sucessfully teach him why everyone needs healthy foods.   INCLUDES A PARENT MANUAL —*Gives parents realistic guidance on common food questions. What to do about picky eaters? What to do about children who just want treats? What about children who keep leaving the table?*

## I Don't Want To Go To The Toilet

TWO STORIES FOR CHILDREN — Katie doesn't want to stop playing to go peepee in the toilet. Ben doesn't want to let his poop out in the toilet. *In two motivating and reassuring stories, the children successfully overcome their resistance*.   INCLUDES A PARENT MANUAL — Learn how to help our kids when they are uninterested, reluctant, and/or fearful.

## I Want To Make Friends

A STORY FOR CHILDREN — Zachary thinks his ideas are the best. He learns how much that bothers the kids. *With the help of his teachers and parents, he becomes a good friend.* INCLUDES A PARENT MANUAL — What to do if your child is bossy, annoying, aggressive, or shy, and/or thin-skinned with peers.

## I'm Getting Ready For Kindergarten

A STORY FOR CHILDREN — Jillian has some worries and questions about going to kindergarten. Through this reasuring story, she begins to feel ready for an exciting year.   INCLUDES A PARENT MANUAL — All of the important academic, social, emotional, and behavorial skills needed for kindergarten are described. Parents will learn how to prepare their kids for all these needed skills.

To order these books: visit www.PerfectingParentingPress.com where you can order online *or* call (810) 388-9500 (M-F 9-5 ET). These 40- to 48- page books are $9.95 each.    All these books are also available at www.Amazon.com.